CONSTITUTION FOR KIDS BILL OF RIGHTS EDITION

2ND GRADE U.S. HISTORY VOL 3

SPEEDY
PUBLISHING

The first ten Amendments to
the Constitution were passed
in 1791 and are collectively
known as the Bill of Rights.

THE FIRST AMENDMENT

grants freedoms concerning religion, expression, assembly, and the right to petition. The Congress shall make no law preventing the establishment of religion or prohibiting its free exercise.

THE SECOND AMENDMENT

protects citizen's right to bear arms. The word arms did not necessarily only mean guns, but it definitely included guns. You may have arms in your home as well as on your person.

THE THIRD
AMENDMENT

prevents the government
from placing troops in
private homes during
war or peace without the
homeowner's permission.

THE FOURTH
AMENDMENT

prevents the government from unreasonable and unlawful search and seizure of the property of US citizens. It requires the government to have a warrant that was issued by a judge.

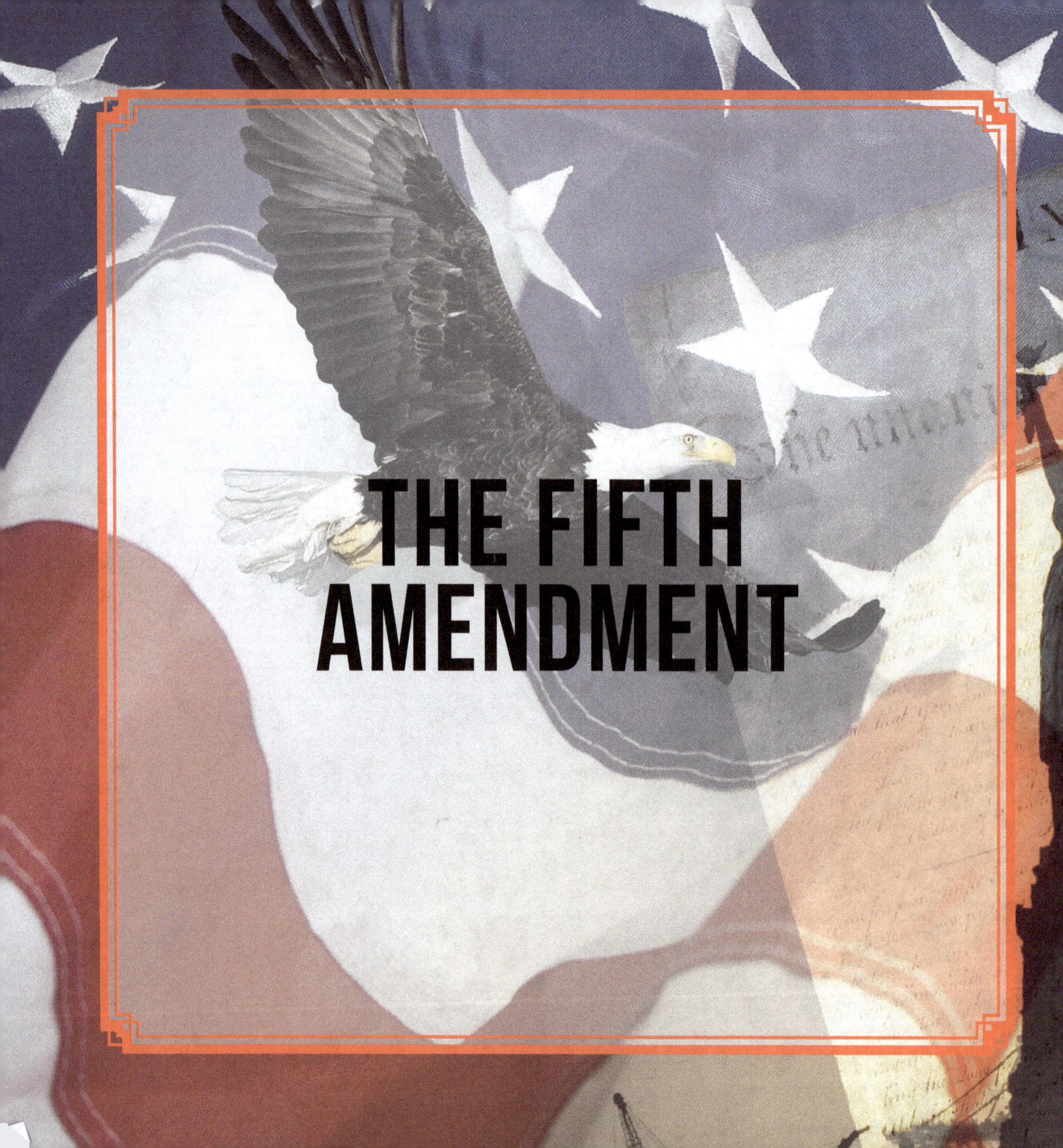
THE FIFTH
AMENDMENT

allows all citizens due
process and the right
to choose not to testify
in court if they feel
their own testimony will
incriminate themselves.

THE SIXTH AMENDMENT

provides a speedy and public trial by a jury for all who are accused of a crime. You have the right to know what you are accused of, to see and hear the people who are witnesses against you and you have the right to a lawyer to help you.

THE SEVENTH AMENDMENT

allows a trial by jury
to be held for certain
civil disputes.

THE EIGHTH AMENDMENT

prevents those accused of excessive bail, excessive fines and suffering cruel and unusual punishments.

THE NINTH AMENDMENT

states that no one's
Constitutional rights should
be used to infringe upon the
rights of another citizen.

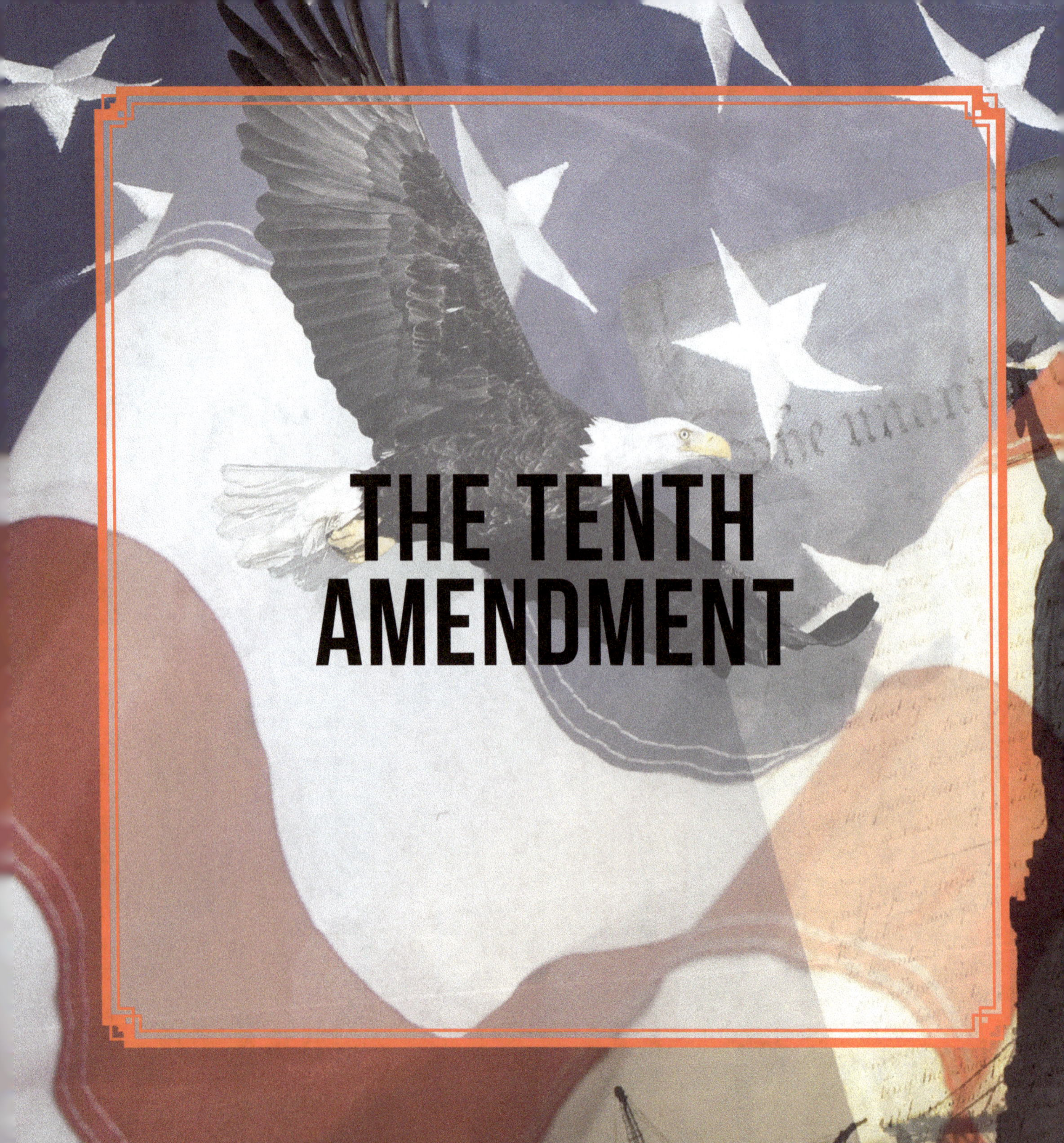

THE TENTH
AMENDMENT

gives all powers not
specifically given to the
United States government
in the Constitution, to either
the states or to the people.

Visit
BABY PROFESSOR
EDUCATION KIDS
www.BabyProfessorBooks.com
to download Free Baby Professor eBooks
and view our catalog of new and exciting
Children's Books